Diet recommendations during blood cancer (leukemia)

Diet can support the affected organs and is not a treatment for the disease. Please check these recommendations always with a nutrition consultant, therapist, doctor or dietician. The recipes and the list of ingredients are supporting the conventional medical therapy.
The calorie disclosures of fresh ingredients (fruit and vegetables) vary according to quality and time of harvest. The contents were checked by a dietician and a nutrition consultant for the Traditional Chinese Medicine (TCM).

Author:
©2017 Josef Miligui
www.ebns.at

AF190383

Source:
The lists are created from the EBNS database for nutritional counseling. The database is used by dietitians, therapists and doctors for advising the patient / client.

Literature:
The specialist literature and the training documents of the German and Austrian dietary and traditional Chinese medicine serve as a knowledge base. We have used the documents as a basis of knowledge, adapted it to our experience and completed them.
http://di-book.com

Title Photo:
©2008 Erika Weixlbaumer

Production and publishing:
BoD – Books on Demand, Norderstedt
ISBN: 9783746025865

Diet recommendations during blood cancer (leukemia)

1   Treatment strategy

Prevention of infection of the gastrointestinal tract (by bacteria, fungi and viruses) and subsequent complications such as. septic infiltration of pathogens into the organism.
If possible, use only foods that are germ-free and spore-free due to a sufficient cooking process. It must be ensured that meat, poultry, eggs, fish or vegetables are thoroughly cooked. Preserves and freeze-dried foods (mashed potatoes, milk powder, instant soups) are a quick alternative.

2   Avoid

- Semi-raw or raw meat and sausage products, breaded meat, meat or sausage salad with mayonnaise, fish that is not cooked (eg smoked fish), breaded fish, fish salads, roast chicken with skin, breaded poultry meat, chicken salads, raw not completely cooked eggs (eg scrambled eggs , Fried eggs, soft eggs, products with mayonnaise, products where raw eggs were processed and not cooked through, tiramisu, hollandaise sauce)
- non-peelable fruit (cherries, grapes, peaches, nectarines, plums, etc.), peelable fruit with bruises and overripe fruits, dried fruit, raw vegetables and salads, mushrooms (eg lettuce, grated carrots, radishes, raw herbs such as Parsley, etc.), unpreserved fruit and vegetable juices
- fresh nuts (high strain of mushroom spores), cereals and oatmeal
- flatulent foods (red cabbage, sauerkraut, beans, peppers, etc.), spicy foods (chili con carne, etc.), very sweet foods, foods and drinks that contain a lot of acidity (citrus juices, tomato soup, foods with a strong vinegar content), fatty foods (Sardines, pork knuckle, etc.), very hard foods (hard rolls, sharp-edged candies

3   Breakfast   kkal. per serving

Banana Soymilk.. 125
Beef broth... 124
Boiled celery salad with exotic spices.. 165
Breakfast - low protein... 575

4   Snack

5   Lunch

6   Afternoon

7   Dinner

8   Any time

9 Recipes

(recommendable) = You can use more.
(little) = You should use less than specified or omit.

9.1 8 treasures of rice

Diuretic, warming the body from the inside, expands blood vessels, strengthens the muscles, regulates internal organs functions, promotes spleen, calms nerves.
Cooking time approx. 1 hour
Calories p. portion: 212
4 portions
Allergens:

Quantity of ingredients:
Lily bulbs 1 table spoon / 5g. (recommended)
Longane 1 table spoon / 5g. (yes)
King Solomon's-seal 1 table spoon / 5g. (yes)
Yam root, yam root tuber 1 table spoon / 5g. (yes)
Coix (seeds) YiYi Ren 1 table spoon / 5g. (yes)
Rice wild (nature rice) 1 1/2 cups / 240g. (yes)
Water 8-10 cups / 800g. (yes)

Cooking instructions:
Each one 1 tbsp: Bai He, Longan, Yu Zhu, Da Zao, Shan Yao, Lian Mi, Yi Yi Ren, Qian Shi
Add hot water and soak for about 30 minutes. Then add 1 - 2 cups of rice (normal) and simmer for 1/2 to 1 hour until the rice is very soft. Or: Cook for about 3 hours with the herbs a congee. Then the herbs do not have to be soaked.

9.2 Artichoke soup

Detoxifying, supports urination, regulates digestion, stimulates appetite, gentle laxative, forcing spleen, promotes weight loss. Strengthens gastrointestinal function, expands blood vessels, prevents cancer.
Cooking time approx. 40 min
Calories p. portion: 142
3 portions
Allergens: GLN

Quantity of ingredients:
Artichoke 4 pieces / 400g. (yes)
Butter organic 1 table spoon / 20g. (yes)
Onion (shallot) 1 piece / 20g. (yes)
Corn flour 1 table spoon / 10g. (yes)
Nutmeg 1 pinch / 0,5g. (yes)
Basic recipe for a vegetable soup (nutritious) 1 cup / 250g. (yes)
Salt 1 pinch / 0,5g. (little)
Lemon 1/4 piece / 8g. (little)
Lemon peel 1/4 piece / g. (yes)
Turmeric (yellow root) 1 pinch / 1g. (recommended)
Sesame paste (Tahini) 1 table spoon / 10g. (yes)
Sesame, white 1 teaspoon / 10g. (little)

Cooking instructions:
Boil the artichokes in 2 liters of water with salt until the outer leaves are light removable. Remove leaves and flower center (fibrous) so that only the soil remains.
Melt the butter, cut the onion into small pieces and steam gently; add some cornmeal, nutmeg; brew with vegetable soup; add salt, a little lemon peel and juice, turmeric and artichoke bottoms, cook gently and puree; Season with Tahin and sprinkle with sesame before serving.

9.3 Banana Soymilk

Good to fight loss of appetite, oral mucosa inflammation. Strengthens body energy, promotes stomach-spleen harmony, promotes digestion, regulates gastrointestinal function. Relieves pain, detoxifying.
Cooking time approx. 5 min
Calories p. portion: 126
2 portions
Allergens: E

Quantity of ingredients:
Banana 1 piece / 120g. (recommended)
Soybean milk 1 1/2 cups / 400g. (yes)
Honey 1 teaspoon / 3g. (yes)
Cinnamon ground 1 pinch / 1g. (yes)
Acerola fruit nectar or powder 1 teaspoon / 2g. (recommended)

Cooking instructions:
Cut the banana into pieces, puree them with soy milk, acerola, honey and cinnamon with the mixing stick.

9.4   Basic recipe for a fish broth

Strengthens the kidneys, promotes watering, reduces blood pressure, strengthens immune system, prevents cancer, reduces radiation damage. Low in cholesterol and protein rich. Improves blood circulation, stimulates appetite.
Cooking time approx. 40 min
Calories p. portion: 128
5 portions
Allergens: DLO

Quantity of ingredients:
Fish pieces mixed (fresh water) 3/4 lbs / 300g. (recommended)
Celery root 1/4 lbs - 4oz / 120g. (yes)
Leek 2 inches / 10g. (yes)
Carrot 2 pieces / 150g. (yes)
White wine 1/2 cup / 125g. (little)
Lemon 1/2 piece / 50g. (little)
Bay leaf 2 leaves / 2g. (yes)
Peppercorns 3 pieces / 2g. (little)
Olive oil 1 table spoon / 10g. (yes)
Water 2 cup / 450g. (yes)

Cooking instructions:
Fry celery, chopped carrots and leeks in olive oil, add bay leaf and peppercorns, add pieces of fish and sauté briefly. Add water, add little white wine or lemon. Simmer gently for 30 minutes. Skim off the resulting foam several times. In the end, sift the ingredients through a cloth.
Refrigerate for later use

9.5   Beef broth

Warming and nourishing, forces.
Cooking time approx. 2-6 hours
Calories p. portion: 125
7 portions
Allergens: L

Quantity of ingredients:
Water 4 cup / 1000g. (yes)
Lemon 2 dashes / 2g. (little)
Beef meat 1,1 lbs / 500g. (yes)
Beef meatbones 2 pieces / 0g. (little)

Turmeric (yellow root) 1 pinch / 1g. (recommended)
Carrot 2 pieces / 100g. (yes)
Celery root 1 inch / 25g. (yes)
Parsley root 1 piece / 150g. (yes)
Onion white 1 piece / 50g. (yes)
Bay leaf 2-3 leaves / 2g. (yes)
Coriander 1/2 teaspoon / 2g. (yes)
Ginger fresh 1 inch / 2g. (little)
Wakame 1 inch / 1g. (yes)
Parsley 1 stem / 10g. (yes)

Cooking instructions:
In a saucepan with water (enough to cover the meat), add a few drops
of lemon juice, a little turmeric, beef and bones, heat till it boils and
simmer for a while; then pour away the whole broth, clean the pot, rinse
off meat and bones with hot water (this will save you from foaming) and
put it back to the saucepan with hot water (amount as you like); add a
good pinch of turmeric, carrot, celery, parsley root to the pot; add onion,
bay leaves, coriander, a piece of sliced ginger, a strip of wakame, a
stalk of parsley; boil everything together and simmer for 2-6 hours (if the
meat is to be used otherwise, take it out of the broth after 1 1/2 - 2
hours, as soon as it is cooked, the bones are returned to the broth);
When the cooking time is over, pour the broth through a sieve and
discard all ingredients.

Notes: The longer the broth has cooked, the warmer but more
nourishing it is. It is after cooling for 3-4 days in the refrigerator durable.
The broth can be drunk hot or used as a base for soups with cereals,
potatoes and fresh vegetables.

9.6 Beetroot soup

Strengthens gastrointestinal function, expands blood vessels,
strengthens the muscles, antioxidativ. Promotes digestion, dissolves
stagnation.
Cooking time approx. 20-30 min
Calories p. portion: 282
4 portions
Allergens: G

Quantity of ingredients:
Olive oil 2 table spoons / 20g. (yes)
Onion white 1 piece chopped / 50g. (yes)
Garlic 1 clove / 2g. (recommended)
Red beet 2,2 lbs (Peeled and diced) / 1000g. (yes)
Cumin (Caraway seed) 1 table spoon / 7g. (yes)
Curcuma 1 teaspoon / 2g. (yes)
Oregano fresh 1 pinch of fresh / 2g. (yes)
Peppers (rose peppers) 1 teaspoon / 2g. (yes)
Créme fraiche cheese 1/4 lbs - 4oz / 125g. (yes)

Cooking instructions:
Heat the oil in a saucepan, fry the onions and garlic in dark brown. Add cumin, turmeric, oregano and salt and deglaze with 1 liter of water. Cook the beetroot for about 20 minutes. Puree the soup and serve in soup bowls with 1 tbsp. creme fraiche. Finally, sprinkle the rose pepper over it.

9.7   Boiled celery salad with exotic spices

Forcing spleen, relieves diarrhea, antibacterial, blood-forming, blood detoxifying, reduces inflammation, diuretic, improves blood circulation.
Cooking time approx. 30 min
Calories p. portion: 166
4 portions
Allergens: GLMNO

Quantity of ingredients:
Celery root 1 1/2 piece / 900g. (yes)
Yogurt (natural, 3.5% fat) 1 cup / 250g. (yes)
Sour cream 15% fat 2 table spoons / 20g. (yes)
Turmeric (yellow root) 1 pinch / 1g. (recommended)
Sesame oil 1 table spoon / 20g. (yes)
Pepper (ground) 1 pinch / 0,5g. (little)
Lemongrass 1 pinch / 1g. (yes)
Onion white 1/2 piece / 25g. (yes)
Mustard 1/2 teaspoon / 1g. (yes)
Black caraway 1 pinch / 1g. (yes)
Salt 1 pinch / 1g. (little)
Lemon juice 1 piece / 40g. (little)
Apple (sour) 1/2 piece / 100g. (yes)
Peppers powder 1 pinch / 1g. (yes)
Vinegar (Apple vinegar) 1 dash / 3g. (yes)

Cooking instructions:
Cook the peeled celeriac in thick slices and then cut into bite-sized strips.

Dressing: Mix a little yoghurt, sour cream, turmeric, sesame oil, pepper, lemongrass powder, finely chopped onion, a little mustard, salt, crushed black cumin, some cold water, lemon juice or vinegar; add the sour chopped apple, some rose paprika, the lukewarm celery and mix well; let it rest for 2 - 3 hours or overnight.

Ideal as a substitute for raw food

9.8 Breakfast - low protein

Increase appetite, detoxifying, increases blood glucose levels, harmonizes heart rhythm, good to fight vomiting, nutritional disorders, diarrhea.
Cooking time approx. 10 min
Calories p. portion: 575
1 portions
Allergens: GO

Quantity of ingredients:
Bread with carob kernel flour 3 oz / 80g. (yes)
Butter organic 1/2 oz / 20g. (yes)
Apricot jam 1 oz / 30g. (recommended)
Fresh cheese with herbs 1 oz / 30g. (yes)
Coffee 1/2 cup / 150g. (yes)
Sugar white 1/2 oz / 10g. (little)

Cooking instructions:
Prepare coffee to taste, make fresh cheese if possible with fresh herbs yourself.

9.9 Breakfast with cheese

Good to fight weakness, stomach pressure, belching, diabetes, acute or chronic obstruction of the bowel, skin problems. Coffee supports urinating, stimulates appetite, detoxifying, increases blood glucose levels, harmonizes heart rhythm.
Cooking time approx. 10 min
Calories p. portion: 593
1 portions
Allergens: AGO

Quantity of ingredients:
Water 1 cup / 120g. (yes)
Coffee 2 teaspoons / 4g. (yes)
Whole grain bread 2 slices / 100g. (recommended)
Margarine 1/2 oz / 10g. (yes)
Edam cheese 1 oz / 30g. (yes)
Strawberry jam 1/2 oz / 20g. (recommended)
Curd cheese 20% 1/8 lbs - 2oz / 40g. (yes)

Cooking instructions:
Prepare coffee as usual. Avoid sugar or use sweetener. Cover the bread slices with margarine and put the cheese and marmalade on the breakfast table. Decorating decoratively increases your appetite.

9.10 Carrot and rice gruel soup

Stops diarrhea, good to fight fever, strengthens immune system, reduces blood pressure.
Cooking time approx. 10 min
Calories p. portion: 101
1 portions
Allergens:

Quantity of ingredients:
Basic recipe for a rice soup (Congee) 1 cup / 120g. (yes)
Carrot 2 pieces / 100g. (yes)
Salt 1 teaspoon / 4g. (little)

Cooking instructions:
Peel and grate carrots. Heat the rice soup (according to the basic recipe) till it boils and add the grated carrots and salt. Cook for 10 minutes.

9.11 Chicken with white turnips on rice

Strengthens bone marrow. Rice to drain the body at overweight and high blood pressure.
Cooking time approx. 45 min
Calories p. portion: 324
4 portions
Allergens: GL

Quantity of ingredients:
Butter organic 2 table spoons / 20g. (yes)
Olive oil 2 table spoons / 20g. (yes)
Onion white 1 piece / 60g. (yes)
Turnips 4 pieces / 200g. (yes)
Garlic 2 pieces / 3g. (recommended)
Basic recipe for a chicken soup (warming) 1 cup / 100g. (little)
Parsley 2 table spoons / 15g. (yes)
Salt 1 pinch / 1g. (little)
Olive oil 1 teaspoon / 4g. (yes)
Chicken meat 7/8 lbs / 400g. (yes)
Water 6 cups / 400g. (yes)
Rice Basmati 1 cup / 120g. (yes)

Cooking instructions:
In a heavy pot, heat the butter and the oil at low temperature. Add the onion, stir and simmer for about 20 minutes on very low heat until soft and golden brown. Add the chopped beets and the chopped garlic cloves and stir well. Add the chicken broth or water, add some salt and heat till it boils. Reduce the heat, put on the lid and simmer the beets for about 20 minutes. Look in between if there is still enough liquid in the pot, and if necessary, pour in a few tablespoons of chicken stock. At the end there should be very little liquid in the pot. Remove the lid and allow the remaining liquid to evaporate, stirring constantly.
In the meantime roast the finely chopped chicken pieces in a frying pan with a little oil. Finally, sprinkle with a little chili and fry for another minute while constantly turning.
Serve the pieces of chicken, turnips and rice on the plates, spread the sauce over them and sprinkle with parsley immediately.
Cook the rice in the ratio of 6 cups of water: 1 cup of rice.
Small, fresh, untreated beets do not need to be peeled. Otherwise, peel beets and place in hot water for 10 minutes. This makes them easier to digest and lose some of their sharp, pungent odor. White turnips are rich in vitamin C, potassium and folic acid.

9.12 Compote from apples

Apple (sweet) stops diarrhea, promotes digestion, appetizing, harmonizes the stomach. Warms stomach and spleen, improves blood circulation.
Cooking time approx. 10 min
Calories p. portion: 67
2 portions
Allergens:

Quantity of ingredients:
Apple (sweet) 1 piece / 220g. (recommended)
Water 1 1/2 cups / 220g. (yes)
Cinnamon ground 1 pinch / 1g. (yes)

Cooking instructions:
Cook the apples (organic) with the skin and seeds. Sprinkle with cinnamon.

9.13 Compote of local fruit and dried fruit

Promotes digestion, supports urination, stops diarrhea, promotes digestion, appetizing, relieves diarrhea. Warms stomach and spleen, improves blood circulation.
Cooking time approx. 15 min
Calories p. portion: 45
4 portions
Allergens:

Quantity of ingredients:
Apple (sweet) 1 piece / 150g. (recommended)
Pear 1 piece / 150g. (little)
Cinnamon ground 1 pinch / 0,2g. (yes)
Lemon peel 1/2 teaspoon / 2g. (yes)
Water 2 cup / 500g. (yes)

Cooking instructions:
Cook the apple and pear with the dried fruit until soft. Sprinkle with cinnamon and lemon zest (organic).

9.14 Cottage cheese with steamed fruit

Good to fight loss of appetite, promotes digestion, supports urination.
Cooking time approx. 20 min
Calories p. portion: 214
2 portions
Allergens: G

Quantity of ingredients:
Cottage cheese 3/4 lbs / 300g. (yes)
Apple (sour) 1 piece / 100g. (yes)
Pear 1 piece / 100g. (little)

Cooking instructions:
Wash apples and pears well, do not peel, and chop small. In a pot with
steam filter, boil them al dente, remove and allow to cool down.
Serve the cheese, spread the fruit on it.

9.15 Cream cheese substitute

Good to fight lactose intolerance. Strengthens body energy, promotes
digestion, promotes weight loss. Good to fight immunodeficiency, loss
of appetite, arteriosclerosis, flatulence, bladder weakness, anemia, high
blood pressure, depressions, diabetes, diarrhea.
Cooking time approx. 20 min
Calories p. portion: 526
2 portions
Allergens: AE

Quantity of ingredients:
Soybean milk 4 cup / 300g. (yes)
Lemon 1 piece / 50g. (little)
Herbs various 2 table spoons / 6g. (yes)
Whole grain bread 6 slices / 300g. (recommended)

Cooking instructions:
Heat the soy milk in a saucepan till it boils, stirring occasionally (gets
burn easily!), Then allow to cool.
Squeeze out the lemon and stir gently under the cooled soy milk
(approx. 80°C/176°F), let it approx. 20 min. rest or clot.
Pour chopped soy milk through a strainer lined with a dishcloth, allow
liquid to drain and then squeeze out remaining liquid with the dishcloth.
Refine to taste with fresh herbs.
Serve with wholemeal bread.

9.16 Fish soup with rosemary

Promotes spleen and liver, reduces blood pressure, strengthens immune system, prevents cancer, reduces radiation damage, has little cholesterol and is protein rich, improves blood circulation, increases appetite. Antioxidant, forcing spleen, dissolves stagnation.
Cooking time approx. 30 min
Calories p. portion: 271
4 portions
Allergens: DLO

Quantity of ingredients:
Basic recipe for a fish soup 2 cup / 500g. (little)
Rosemary 1/2 bunch / 7g. (yes)
Onion (spring onion) 1 piece / 20g. (yes)
Olive oil 2 table spoons / 35g. (yes)
Fish pieces mixed (fresh water) 5/8 lbs - 8oz / 250g. (recommended)
Carrot 1 piece / 120g. (yes)
Parsnip 1 piece / 180g. (yes)
Celery root 1 slice / 20g. (yes)
Salt 1 pinch / 1g. (little)
Peppercorns 2 pieces / 1g. (little)
Garlic 1 clove / 3g. (recommended)

Cooking instructions:
Fry the onion and garlic in oil. Add fish broth. Add diced carrots, parsnips and celery. Season with salt and peppercorns. Simmer the soup on a low heat for 25 minutes.
Wash the fish, drizzle with lemon juice, divide into pieces and add to the soup with the pink rosemary. Cook for 5 min on low heat.
Add the chives and parsley and season the soup with the salt.

9.17 Fish soup with white wine, laurel and marjoram

Strengthens the kidneys, promotes watering, promotes spleen and liver, reduces blood pressure, improves blood circulation, improves medication effect, stimulates appetite, reduces blood pressure.
Cooking time approx. 45 min
Calories p. portion: 200
3 portions
Allergens: DLO

Quantity of ingredients:
Onion (spring onion) 2 pieces / 40g. (yes)
Garlic 1 clove / 2g. (recommended)
Basic recipe for a fish soup 2 cup / 500g. (little)
Carrot 1 piece / 60g. (yes)
Parsnip 1 piece / 100g. (yes)
Celery root 1 slice / 60g. (yes)
Salt 1 pinch / 1g. (little)
Peppercorns 2 pieces / 1g. (little)
Lemon 1/4 piece / 10g. (little)
White wine 1/2 cup / 125g. (little)
Bay leaf 2 leaves / 1g. (yes)
Rosemary 1 teaspoon / 2g. (yes)
Chives 1 teaspoon (chopped) / 3g. (yes)
Parsley 1 teaspoon (chopped) / 3g. (yes)

Cooking instructions:
Fry the onion and garlic in oil until translucent. Add fish broth. Add the diced carrot, parsnip and celery. Season with salt and peppercorns. Simmer the soup on a low heat for 25 minutes.
Wash the fish, drizzle with lemon juice, divide into pieces and add to the soup with the wine, the bay leaves and the marjoram. Cook for 5 min on low heat.
Add the chives and parsley and season the soup with the salt.

9.18 Grilled lamb chops with sweetpotatorpuree and leafy vegetables

Relieves weakness, strengthens lung, spleen and stomach.
Strengthens the immune system, reduces fat, improves digestion.
Cooking time approx. 45 min
Calories p. portion: 914
2 portions
Allergens: E

Quantity of ingredients:
Lamb meat 6 pieces (chops) / 300g. (yes)
Garlic 2 cloves / 3g. (recommended)
Rosemary 2 table spoons / 5g. (yes)
Salt 1 pinch / 1g. (little)
Olive oil 2 table spoons / 20g. (yes)

Sweet potato 3/4 lbs / 300g. (yes)
Basil 1 table spoon / 3g. (yes)
Soybean milk 1/4 lbs - 4oz / 100g. (yes)
Basil 1 table spoon / 3g. (yes)
Salt 1 pinch / 1g. (little)
Nutmeg 1 pinch / 0,5g. (yes)
Pepper (ground) 1 pinch / 0,5g. (little)
Chard 2 handful / 20g. (yes)
Spinach 2 handful / 20g. (yes)
Savoy cabbage / kale 2 handful / 20g. (yes)
White cabbage 2 handful / 20g. (yes)
Herbs various Handful / 10g. (yes)
Olive oil 2 table spoons / 20g. (yes)
Salt 1 pinch / 1g. (little)
Pepper (ground) 1 pinch / 0,5g. (little)

Cooking instructions:
Lamb chops:
Preheat the oven grill to about 180°C/365°F and set the shelf to a
height, such that the chops are about 8 to 12 centimeters from the heat
source. Remove the most fat of the chops and place them in a fireproof
mold. Rub the meat first with garlic, then with the rosemary salt mixture
and spread a few teaspoons of olive oil over it.
Turn the lamb chops once so that they are covered with oil on both
sides, put them under the grill and grill on both sides for 5 to 7 minutes
or until the meat is well browned.

Mashed sweet potatoes:
Peel all sweet potatoes and cut into large cubes, boil gently in salted
water and strain. Leave to soak in the 100°C/212°F hot brook for a few
minutes. Remove the basil leaves. Puree sweet potatoes.
Approximately Boil 1/8 l soymilk with basil once, then strain a little and
strain and mix with the passed sweet potatoes. Season with salt,
pepper and nutmeg. Depending on the consistency of the puree, add a
little more milk.

Steamed leafy vegetables:
After the season chard, spinach, savoy cabbage, white cabbage, fresh
herbs and the mugwort in a pot with olive oil softly. Season with salt and
pepper

9.19 Grilled salmon steaks with cauliflower and potatoes

Improves digestion, regenerates skin, supports urination, lowers cholesterol, supports digestion.
Cooking time approx. 30 min
Calories p. portion: 330
4 portions
Allergens: D

Quantity of ingredients:
Garlic 1 clove / 1g. (recommended)
Onion (shallot) 1/2 piece / 5g. (yes)
Lemon juice 1 dash / 1g. (little)
Salt 1 pinch / 1g. (little)
Cauliflower 1 piece / 500g. (yes)
Olive oil 2 table spoons / 20g. (yes)
Garlic 1 clove / 1g. (recommended)
Water 2/3 cup / g. (yes)
Parsley 2 table spoons / 15g. (yes)
Potato 1,1 lbs / 500g. (yes)
Salt 1 pinch / 1g. (little)
Salmon 4 pieces (steaks) / 500g. (little)
Lemon 1/2 piece / 2g. (little)

Cooking instructions:
Garlic shallots mixture:
Finely squeeze the garlic, finely chop the shallots, add a dash of lemon juice and salt and stir. Mix with a little oil to a paste.

Cauliflower:
Cut the cauliflower into pieces.
Heat the oil in a heavy saucepan and fry the crushed garlic for a short time.
Add the cauliflower pieces and turn in the oil. Add a little water and cook until the cauliflower is firm. Strain the cauliflower and cook the remaining water until a thick sauce remains. Add the cauliflower and crush it roughly with a wooden spoon. Add the chopped parsley and salt.

Potatoes:
Cook the potato in a saucepan with plenty of water, strain and peel.

Salmon Steak:
Preheat the oven at about 180°C/356°F. Rub in the salmon slices with the garlic-scarlet mixture and grill as close as possible to the heat source for 4 to 8 minutes from both sides. You are done when the meat is easy to divide when you pierce with a fork.

Serve and sprinkle with lemon slices and the chopped parsley.

9.20 Grilled tofu with rice noodles, spinach and sugar snaps

Reduces flatulence. Supports urination, detoxifying. Good to fight blood circulation disorders. Strengthens gastrointestinal function, expands blood vessels, stimulates appetite. Promotes bowel movement, improves blood circulation.
Cooking time approx. 30 min
Calories p. portion: 327
4 portions
Allergens: E

Quantity of ingredients:
Sake 1/3 cup / 85g. (yes)
Sugar cane sugar 1 table spoon / 7g. (little)
Garlic 5 cloves / 7g. (recommended)
Onion (spring onion) 3 pieces / 60g. (yes)
Ginger fresh 1 inch / 5g. (little)
Rapeseed oil 2 table spoons / 20g. (yes)
Spinach 2 handful / 30g. (yes)
Peas, green 7/8 lbs / 400g. (yes)
Water 1 table spoon / g. (yes)
Rice noodles 1 package / 250g. (yes)
Water 4 cup / g. (yes)
Basil 1 table spoon / 3g. (yes)
Soy Tofu 1,1 lbs / 500g. (yes)

Cooking instructions:
In a medium bowl mix together: Tamari souce, rice wine, sugar, crushed garlic, spring onion, grated ginger, chopped basil and the rapeseed oil. Add the tofu and leave in the marinade for at least 1 hour. Cover the mangetout peas in a pan with a little water, lightly simmer 5 min. Add the spinach and steam again 3 min.

Cook the rice noodles according to manufacturer's instructions, drain, rinse again with warm water and drain.

Preheat the grill or oven grill, grill the tofu for 5 minutes on both sides and set aside.

Arrange the pasta on the plates, divide the vegetables all around and place the tofu over the noodles. Douse with the marinade.

9.21 Halibut with tomato and garlic sauce

Promotes digestion, helps to digest fat, supports urination, reduces blood pressure, good to fight rheumatism, flatulence, bladder weakness, anemia, high blood pressure, depressions, diabetes, diarrhea. Valuable omega-3 fatty acids.
Cooking time approx. 45 min
Calories p. portion: 319
5 portions
Allergens: D

Quantity of ingredients:
Rice variety any 1 cup / 120g. (yes)
Water 6 cups / 240g. (yes)
Salt 1 pinch / 1g. (little)
Halibut (Flatfish) 2,2 lbs / 800g. (yes)
Salt 1 pinch / 1g. (little)
Pepper (ground) 1 pinch / 0,5g. (little)
Lemon juice 1 dash / 2g. (little)
Bay leaf 2 pieces / 2g. (yes)
Lemon 1 piece / 30g. (little)
Garlic 8 pieces / 10g. (recommended)
Thyme dried 1 table spoon / 5g. (yes)
Olives 0,2 lbs / 75g. (yes)
Tomato 4 pieces / 200g. (yes)
Salt 1 pinch / 1g. (little)
Pepper (ground) 1 pinch / 0,5g. (little)

Cooking instructions:
Cook rice with salted water (1:3).
Rinse the fish under running cold water, dab with kitchen paper and rub with salt, pepper and lemon juice.
Place the fish fillets in a casserole dish with pieces of bay leaf.

Wash the lemon hot and cut into slices, peel and halve the garlic.
Sprinkle the olives and the thyme over them.
Brew the tomatoes with hot water, skin and chop.

Mix all ingredients, season with salt and pepper and distribute around the fish.

Cook everything at 200°C/392°F for about 20 minutes.
Serve with the rice.

9.22 Hearty polenta mash

Strengths spleen and stomach, promotes watering, promotes digestion, detoxifying, promotes perspiration, reduces blood lipids, stimulates, dissolves stagnation, stimulates appetite, dissolves stagnation.
Cooking time approx. 10 min
Calories p. portion: 262
2 portions
Allergens:

Quantity of ingredients:
Corn Grease (Polenta) 1 cup / 120g. (yes)
Onion (spring onion) 2 pieces / 40g. (yes)
Ginger fresh 1/2 teaspoon / 2g. (little)
Nutmeg 1 pinch / 1g. (yes)
Salt 1 pinch / 1g. (little)
Olive oil 1 table spoon / 10g. (yes)
Turmeric (yellow root) 1 pinch / 1g. (recommended)
Water 1 1/2 cups / 240g. (yes)

Cooking instructions:
Stir in the polenta in boiling water and let it swell for 7 min. Add green onion, grated ginger, turmeric, nutmeg, salt and olive oil and wait for 3 more minutes.

9.23 Leek and potato gratin

Reduces inflammation, improves digestion, regenerates skin, supports urination, lowers cholesterol, promotes sweating, dissolves stagnation.
Cooking time approx. 1 hour
Calories p. portion: 368
4 portions
Allergens: CGL

Quantity of ingredients:
Potato 1,1 lbs / 500g. (yes)
Leek 1,1 lbs / 500g. (yes)
Apple (sour) 1 piece / 200g. (yes)
Créme fraiche cheese 1/4 lbs - 4oz / 125g. (yes)
Basic recipe for a vegetable soup (nutritious) 1/4 cup / 20g. (yes)
Chicken yolk 1 piece / 20g. (little)
Emmental cheese 2 table spoons / 20g. (yes)
Salt 1 pinch / 1g. (little)
Pepper (ground) 1 pinch / 0,5g. (little)

Cooking instructions:
Wash the potatoes, peel, cut into very thin slices and pat dry. Place half in a flat greased baking dish.
Clean and wash leeks and cut into fine rings. Wash apple, peel and cut into thin slices. Spread the leek rings and apple slices on top. Put the remaining potato slices on top.
Mix crème fraîche, egg yolk, grated Emmentaler, salt and pepper, if necessary add some vegetable stock and pour over the casserole.
Bake at 200°C/392°F in the oven for about 45 to 50 minutes until golden brown. Cover with parchment paper after 30 minutes to prevent the burr from drying out.

9.24 Melanzani with olive oil and turmeric

improves blood circulation, reduces inflammation, relieves pain, promotes digestion, helps to digest fat, supports urination, reduces blood pressure.
Cooking time approx. 30 min
Calories p. portion: 432
2 portions
Allergens: A

Quantity of ingredients:
Aubergine 2 pieces / 300g. (yes)
Olive oil 4 table spoons / 60g. (yes)
Tomato 4 pieces / 200g. (yes)
Turmeric (yellow root) 1/2 teaspoon / 1g. (recommended)
Ground 1 pinch / 1g. (yes)
Salt 1 pinch / 1g. (little)
White bread (wheat bread) 4 slices / 80g. (little)

Cooking instructions:
Cut the melanzani into slices and spread them with the tomatoes on a baking tray. Sprinkle with olive oil and then with turmeric, caraway and salt. Bake them in the tube 20 min.
Serve with the white bread.

9.25 Noodle casserole with plugs and peaches

Relieves fatigue, relaxes, good to fight belching, acute or chronic obstruction of the bowel, flatulence, heartburn. Calms nerves and stomach, strengthens the defense, good to fight fungi infections.
Cooking time approx. 1 hour
Calories p. portion: 442
4 portions
Allergens: ACGO

Quantity of ingredients:
Peaches 1,1 lbs / 500g. (little)
Noodles (wheat, ribbon noodles) with egg 5/8 oz / 200g. (yes)
Chicken egg 2 pieces / 120g. (little)
Sugar - icing sugar 1/8 lbs - 2oz / 40g. (little)
Vanilla sugar natural 3 package / 3g. (yes)
Lemon peel 1/2 piece / 2g. (yes)
Cinnamon ground 1/4 teaspoon / 1g. (yes)
Curd cheese 20% 5/8 lbs - 8oz / 250g. (yes)
Butter organic 2 teaspoons / 8g. (yes)
Strawberry jam 4 table spoons / 50g. (recommended)

Cooking instructions:
Preheat oven to 180°C/356°F.
Put Peaches briefly in boiling water, drain and peel off the skin. Cut peaches into small slices.
Cook noodles in plenty of salted water until firm, drain, chill off cold and drain.
Separate eggs. Stir egg yolks with icing sugar, vanilla sugar, grated lemon zest and cinnamon until fluffy with the whisk. Stir in the curd cheese. Add the noodles.
Beat the egg whites into firm snow and carefully lift them under the pasta. Spread a baking dish thinly with butter. Alternating pate noodle mixture and peach slices into the form layers. Finish with the pasta mixture. Sprinkle the casserole with butter flakes and bake in a preheated oven for 3o minutes.
Serve portion by portion with a tablespoon of jam.

9.26 Potato-basil soup

Reduces inflammation, improves digestion, supports urination, lowers cholesterol, reduces blood pressure, strengthens immune system, prevents cancer, reduces radiation damage, antioxidativ, dissolves stagnation.
Cooking time approx. 25 min
Calories p. portion: 96
4 portions
Allergens: L

Quantity of ingredients:
Water 2 cups / 450g. (yes)
Potato 4 pieces / 200g. (yes)
Carrot 2 pieces / 100g. (yes)
Celery root 1 piece / 500g. (yes)
Pepper (ground) 1 pinch / 0,5g. (little)
Ground 1 pinch / 1g. (yes)
Garlic 1 clove / 3g. (recommended)
Salt 1 pinch / 1g. (little)
Lemon 1 teaspoon / 3g. (little)
Basil (fresh) 1 Bunch / 50g. (yes)
Peppers powder 1 pinch / 1g. (yes)
Sugar cane sugar 1 pinch / 1g. (little)
Olive oil 1 table spoon / 10g. (yes)

Cooking instructions:
Peeled and chopped 4 medium potatoes in a pot of hot water and 2 chopped medium carrots, a piece of celery root, a pinch of pepper, a pinch of ground cumin, crushed a small clove of garlic, a pinch of salt, 1 teaspoon of lemon juice, simmer until the Vegetables is soft.

Add 1 bunch finely chopped basil into one half of the soup and puree everything; stir in the other half of the basil; with rose paprika, a pinch of whole cane sugar, 1 tablespoon of olive oil or butter, freshly ground pepper, salt to taste.

9.27 Provencal noodle pan

Improves blood circulation, reduces Inflammation, relieves pain, strengthens the muscles, tendons and bones, diuretic, supports urination.
Cooking time approx. 45 min
Calories p. portion: 196
2 portions
Allergens: ACL

Quantity of ingredients:
Noodles (whole grain) with egg 5/8 oz / 200g. (yes)
Aubergine 1/8 lbs - 2oz / 60g. (yes)
Zucchini 1/8 lbs - 2oz / 60g. (yes)
Peppers 1/8 lbs - 2oz / 50g. (yes)
Beef meat 1/8 lbs - 2oz / 50g. (yes)
Garlic 2 pieces / 4g. (recommended)
Rapeseed oil 1/8 oz / 5g. (yes)
Basic recipe for a vegetable soup (nutritious) 1/4 cup / 60g. (yes)
Tomato juice 1/3 cup / 75g. (yes)
Oregano fresh 1 pinch / 1g. (yes)
Rosemary 1 pinch / 1g. (yes)
Pepper (ground) 1 pinch / 0,5g. (little)
Salt 1 pinch / 0,5g. (little)

Cooking instructions:
Boil noodles in plenty of salted water, chill and drain.
Wash vegetables, dice aubergine and zucchini.
Core the pepper and cut into cubes of approx. 1 cm.
Braise garlic, minced beef and prepared vegetables in heated oil, pour in vegetable stock and tomato juice and finish cooking.
Add pasta to the sauce.
Heat the whole and season with the spices and salt.

9.28 Pumpkin curry

Promotes digestion and sweating, Dissolves stagnation, strengthens lungs and spleen, diuretic, reduces blood glucose, forcing spleen and digestive system, detoxifying, strengthens the muscles and bones.
Cooking time approx. 20 min
Calories p. portion: 193
3 portions
Allergens:

Quantity of ingredients:
Pumpkin 3/4 lbs / 300g. (yes)
Olive oil 2 table spoons / 30g. (yes)
Coriander 1 pinch / 1g. (yes)
Pepper (ground) 1 pinch / 0,5g. (little)
Curry 1 pinch / 1g. (yes)
Water 1/4 cup / 50g. (yes)
Salt 1 pinch / 1g. (little)
Parsley 1 table spoon / 7g. (yes)
Cardamom 1 pinch / 1g. (yes)
Turmeric (yellow root) 1 pinch / 1g. (recommended)
Rice (whole grain) 1/2 cup / 60g. (yes)
Water 3 cups / 300g. (yes)
Salt 1 pinch / 1g. (little)

Cooking instructions:
Heat olive oil in pan. Steam the pumpkin cut in cubes, season with cilantro, pepper and curry, simmer with a little water, salt with sea salt, add chopped parsley with cardamom and turmeric, simmer on a small fire for about 10 minutes, depending on the pumpkin, the pumpkin should still be firm.
Place the rice in salted water, bring to the boil and let it simmer over low heat for about 15 minutes.

9.29 Pumpkin slices with spicy rice

Strengthens lungs and spleen, diuretic, reduces blood glucose, protects liver, for the drainage of the body overweight and high blood pressure, harmonizes liver.
Cooking time approx. 45 min
Calories p. portion: 438
4 portions
Allergens: AG

Quantity of ingredients:
Clarified butter 1/2 teaspoon / 5g. (little)
Saffron 1 Sachet / 0,1g. (yes)
Turmeric (yellow root) 1 teaspoon / 2g. (recommended)
Rice Basmati 1 cup / 120g. (yes)
Water 1 cup / 120g. (yes)
Salt 1/2 teaspoon / 2g. (little)
Pumpkin 6-8 slices / 400g. (yes)
Barley flour 1 cup / 10g. (yes)

Breadcrumbs (wheat bread, bread roll) 1 cup / 10g. (yes)
Salt 1/2 teaspoon / 2g. (little)
Pepper (ground) 1 pinch / 1g. (little)
Butter organic 1 table spoon / 10g. (yes)
Cream, sweet 30% 1 1/2 cup / 300g. (little)
Barley flour 2 table spoons / 20g. (yes)
Chives 2 table spoons / 20g. (yes)
Dill 2 table spoons / 20g. (yes)

Cooking instructions:
Melt the fat in a small saucepan, add saffron and turmeric, lightly roast over medium heat for about 1-2 minutes to allow the aromas to develop (note: the spices should never be burnt). Add the rice for about 2 minutes stir fry, add the salt, stir briefly and add the water, stir and close the pot with a lid. Cook at low to medium heat until the water is almost completely absorbed, then remove from the heat and set aside with the lid still closed and let it swell. Do not stir! When the water is completely absorbed, the rice is ready!
Mix flour, bread crumbs, salt and pepper. Moisten the pumpkin slices with water or mashed egg, turn the slices in the flour mixture and fry gently in butter until golden brown and the pumpkin is soft. Melt the butter in a small saucepan, brown the barley flour in it and remove from heat, add the sour cream, season with salt, pepper, add the chopped herbs and pour the sauce over the fried pumpkin slices. Serve with the rice.

9.30 Rhubarb and apple jelly

Antioxidants, lots of vitamin C, laxative, relieves pain, detoxifying, warms stomach and spleen, improves blood circulation.
Cooking time approx. 15 min
Calories p. portion: 180
2 portions
Allergens:

Quantity of ingredients:
Rhubarb 5/8 oz / 200g. (yes)
Apple juice (natural cloudy) 1 cup / 300g. (recommended)
Corn starch 1 oz / 30g. (yes)
Honey 1/2 oz / 20g. (yes)
Vanilla sugar natural 1 pinch / 0,5g. (yes)
Cinnamon ground 1 pinch / 0,5g. (yes)
Peppermint 2 leaves / 2g. (yes)

Cooking instructions:
Add the cornstarch to a 1/2 cup apple juice.
Simmer the rhubarb in 1 cup of water for 10 min.
Add the remaining apple juice and the cornstarch, stir, heat till it boils again.
Sweet with honey and season with vanilla and cinnamon. Spread the mixture on dessert bowls and garnish with mint.

9.31 Ricepudding

Regulates gastrointestinal function. Strengthens spleen and stomach, strengthens the muscles. Vitamin C rich.
Cooking time approx. 2 hours and more
Calories p. portion: 316
1 portions
Allergens: G

Quantity of ingredients:
Cow's milk (whole milk 3.5% fat) 3/4 cup - 6 oz / 200g. (yes)
Rice round grain 1 oz / 25g. (yes)
Banana 1/4 lbs - 4oz / 100g. (recommended)
Red berry (without sugar) 2 teaspoons / 4g. (little)

Cooking instructions:
Heat half of the milk till it boils in a small saucepan.
Sprinkle the rice and cook on low heat for about 15 minutes.
Peel the banana, finely grate with the blender and add the beetroot juice.
Mix the banana bran under the hot rice.
Pour a pudding mold (about 1/4 liter of contents) in cold water.
Fill the banana rice in the mold and let the pudding swell at room temperature.
After about 3 hours it is solid and can be toppled.
Take the remaining milk as a drink.

9.32 Roasted millet with plum compote

Supports urination, promotes spleen and kidney, strengthens the defense. Good to fight fungi infections.
Cooking time approx. 30 min
Calories p. portion: 139
4 portions
Allergens:

Quantity of ingredients:
Millet 1 cup / 120g. (little)
Water 1 1/2 cups / 250g. (yes)
Plum 1 1/2 cups / 250g. (little)
Vanilla pod 1 pinch / 1g. (yes)
Water 5/8 lbs - 8oz / 250g. (yes)
Cinnamon ground 1 pinch / 1g. (yes)
Acerola fruit nectar or powder 1/2 teaspoon / 1g. (recommended)

Cooking instructions:
Roast millet briefly, pour over water, heat till it boils and let stand for 20 min. to swell.

Cook plums with water, vanilla and cinnamon 10 min. then strain. Add acerola and add to the millet.

9.33 Semolina porridge with banana

Regulates gastrointestinal function, reduces inflammation, antiallergic, good to fight blood circulation disorders.
Cooking time approx. 15 min
Calories p. portion: 307
1 portions
Allergens: AG

Quantity of ingredients:
Cow's milk (whole milk 3.5% fat) 3/4 cup - 6 oz / 200g. (yes)
Spelled semolina 2 table spoons / 30g. (yes)
Butter organic 1 teaspoon / 4g. (yes)
Banana 1/2 piece / 50g. (recommended)

Cooking instructions:
Heat the half of the milk in a small pot. Add the semolina and boil it shortly in the milk. Let it swell at low heat for 3 minutes with constant stirring. Remove the pot from the heat, add the remaining milk with the snow bean and place the mush in a small bowl. Add the butter and the battered banana.
For adults, a pinch of cinnamon can be spread over it.

9.34 Sliced lamb with rosemary potatoes

Improves digestion, regenerates skin, supports urination, lowers cholesterol, reduces blood pressure, strengthens immune system. Strengthens gastrointestinal function, expands blood vessels.
Cooking time approx. 1 hour
Calories p. portion: 461
4 portions
Allergens: LO

Quantity of ingredients:
Lamb meat 7/8 lbs - 1 lbs / 500g. (yes)
Olive oil 2 table spoons / 20g. (yes)
Onion white 1 piece / 50g. (yes)
Garlic 1 clove / 2g. (recommended)
Nutmeg 1 pinch / 0,2g. (yes)
Carrot 3 pieces / 150g. (yes)
Celery root 1/4 tuber / 120g. (yes)
Rosemary 1 Twig / 3g. (yes)
Savory 1 teaspoon / 2g. (yes)
Parsley 1 table spoon / 8g. (yes)
Pepper powder (hot) 1 pinch / 2g. (yes)
Red wine 1/2 cup / 125g. (little)
Salt (herbal) 1 pinch / 1g. (little)
Lemon juice 1/2 piece / 15g. (little)
Cranberry 1 table spoon / 10g. (yes)
Potato 6 pieces / 400g. (yes)

Cooking instructions:
Cut the lamb into strips, cut the carrots and celery into small cubes. Heat the olive oil in a pan, fry the lamb in it, add the cut onions and garlic, salt with herbal salt, a little water, parsley, deglaze with red wine, season with paprika and small cut rosemary, mugwort, savory, carrots and celery, turn the heat back on small Simmer for about 35 minutes. Season with pepper and nutmeg, if necessary still salt, add a little lemon juice, season with paprika, cranberries.

Cut the potatoes in half, the length of, spread a little olive oil on the cut surface, salt, sprinkle 2-3 rosemary needles on each half potato, place the potatoes on the baking sheet and bake in a preheated oven for approx. 25 minutes at 190°C/374°F.

9.35 Spicy Tofu Vegetable Pan

Forcing spleen, relieves constipation, detoxifying, reduces inflammation, improves blood circulation, promotes sweating, dissolves stagnation, reduces flatulence, reduces blood pressure, strengthens immune system, prevents cancer, reduces radiation damage.
Cooking time approx. 25 min
Calories p. portion: 241
4 portions
Allergens: EN

Quantity of ingredients:
Sesame oil 2 table spoons / 20g. (yes)
Carrot 2 pieces / 100g. (yes)
Fennel 1 piece / 250g. (yes)
Leek 1 piece / 200g. (yes)
Salt 1 pinch / 1g. (little)
Turmeric (yellow root) 1 pinch / 1g. (recommended)
Lemon juice 1 dach / 1g. (little)
Soy Tofu 1 package / 120g. (yes)
Pepper (ground) 1 pinch / 0,5g. (little)
Soy sauce 1 dash / 3g. (yes)
Rice (whole grain) 1 cup / 120g. (yes)
Water 6 cups / 500g. (yes)
Salt 1 pinch / 1g. (little)

Cooking instructions:
Heat sesame oil in a hot wok or a hot pan; fry the chopped carrots, fennel and leek slices; salt, a dash of lemon juice, turmeric, tofu cubes roast for 1 - 2 minutes.
Add the pepper and cook covered for about 5 minutes; drizzle with soy sauce. Place the rice in salted water, heat till it boils and let it simmer over low heat for about 15 minutes.

9.36 Spinach with cottage cheese

Improves digestion, regenerates skin, supports urination, lowers cholesterol. Promotes bowel movement, improves blood circulation, forcing spleen and bowel, improves pancreatic function. Strengthens gastrointestinal function.
Cooking time approx. 10 min
Calories p. portion: 263
1 portions
Allergens: GN

Quantity of ingredients:
Sesame oil 1 table spoon / 10g. (yes)
Onion white 1/2 piece / 40g. (yes)
Garlic 1/2clove / 1g. (recommended)
Spinach 2 handful / 150g. (yes)
Pepper (ground) 1 pinch / 0,2g. (little)
Nutmeg 1 pinch / 0,2g. (yes)
Salt 1 pinch / 0,5g. (little)
Potato 4 pieces / 200g. (yes)
Sour cream 15% fat 2 table spoons / g. (yes)
Salt 1 pinch / 0,3g. (little)

Cooking instructions:
Heat in a pot sesame oil, add finely chopped onion, roast glassy; fry a little garlic; stew in strips of spinach for about 3 minutes; add ground pepper, nutmeg, salt, a bit of sour cream as desired or serve the spinach with a large dollop of cottage cheese as an appetizer.
In addition, boil the potatoes in salted water, then peel.

9.37 Tea from elderberry blossom tea

Good, if you have a sore throat. Good to fight colds. Promotes urination, good to fight flu, urinary stones, concentration weakness, blackheads, hay fever, rheumatism. Strengthen the immune system, diaphoretic.
Cooking time approx. 10 min
Calories p. portion: 7
4 portions
Allergens:

Quantity of ingredients:
Elderberry blossom tee 4 teaspoons / 12g. (recommended)
Water 2 cup / 500g. (yes)

Cooking instructions:
Heat the water till it boils and put it aside. Add elderberry blossom tea and 10 min. to let go. Sweet to taste with honey. Strain when pouring.

9.38 Tea from wormwood herb

Good to fight general weakness, flatulence, stomach weakness, bad breath, bile complaints, jaundice, kidney weakness, earache, open wounds. Improves circulation, promotes menstruation.
Cooking time approx. 5 min
Calories p. portion: 0
1 portions
Allergens:

Quantity of ingredients:
Wormwood 1 teaspoon / 2g. (recommended)
Water 1 cup / 120g. (yes)

Cooking instructions:
Take 2 teaspoons of wormwood herb and pour over 250 ml of boiling water. Let it rest for three minutes, then sift it. Drink half an hour before eating.

9.39 Tea from yarrow

Blood detoxifying, blood stilling, cramp-dissolving, improves digestion, good to fight flatulence, diabetes, diarrhea, constipation, bleeding.
Cooking time approx. 15 min
Calories p. portion: 0
2 portions
Allergens:

Quantity of ingredients:
Yarrow tea 2-4 teaspoons / 6g. (recommended)
Water 2 cup / 500g. (yes)

Cooking instructions:
Heat the water till it boils and put it aside. Add yarrow and 10 min. to let go. Strain. Sweet to taste with honey.

9.40 Tea Green tea

Green tea promotes digestion, supports urination, dissolves mucus, detoxifying, stimulates nerves, reduces blood lipids, lowers cholesterol, reduces inflammation.
Cooking time approx. 10 min
Calories p. portion: 2
1 portions
Allergens:

Quantity of ingredients:
Green tea 1 teaspoon / 2g. (recommended)
Water 1 cup / 120g. (yes)

Cooking instructions:
For each cup you use a teaspoonful or a teabag.
Pour green tea only with 60 to 80 ° C / 140 to 176 °F hot water, otherwise it will be bitter.
If the tea has a stimulating effect, let it draw for two to three minutes. It has a calming effect for a duration of five minutes (no longer, otherwise it will be bitter!).
Another method: Pour the tea leaves with about 70 ° C / 158 °F hot water and pour the water immediately again. Then just pour hot water again. The bitter substances disappear and the tea gets a milder aroma.

9.41 Tea mixture appetizing

Ginger powder is warming, promotes sweating, dissolves stagnation.
Cooking time approx. 10 min
Calories p. portion: 0
4 portions
Allergens:

Quantity of ingredients:
Bitter orange peel 1 teaspoons / 3g. (yes)
Yarrow tea 1 teaspoons / 3g. (recommended)
Ginger powder 1g. Or 0,034oz / 1g. (yes)
Horehound leaves 1 teaspoons / 3g. (yes)
Water 2 cups / 500g. (yes)

Cooking instructions:
Brew one tablespoon of tea mixture with half a liter of water and leave for 10 min. to let go. Then strain and drink in small sips before eating.

9.42 Turkey rolls in tomato cream

Improves digestion, lowers cholesterol, strengthens blood, strengthens bone marrow, good to fight high blood pressure, helps to digest fat.
Cooking time approx. 30 min
Calories p. portion: 301
2 portions
Allergens: G

Quantity of ingredients:
Champignon 1/4 lbs - 4oz / 100g. (yes)
Turkey breast meat 5/8 oz / 200g. (yes)
Turkey ham 1/4 lbs - 4oz / 100g. (yes)
Olive oil 2 teaspoons / 6g. (yes)
Tomato 1 piece / 60g. (yes)
Cream, sweet 30% 2 table spoons / 20g. (little)
Garlic 1 piece / 2g. (recommended)
Salt 1 pinch / 1g. (little)
Pepper (ground) 1 pinch / 0,5g. (little)
Basil (fresh) 1 table spoon / 5g. (yes)
Potato 5/8 oz / 200g. (yes)

Cooking instructions:
Cook potatoes in salted water and peel.
Cut the turkey into schnitzel. Thoroughly clean the mushrooms, rub them and cut them into slices. Spread the mushrooms and boiled ham over the turkey schnitzel. Roll up the schnitzel, fix with a toothpick and fry in oil for about 8-10 minutes from all sides, possibly add some liquid. Briefly dip the meat tomato in boiling water, skin, halve, remove seeds and dice the pulp. Put in the pan. Braise briefly. Add the cream to the turkey rolls and tomato pieces. Heat till it boil.
Season with garlic, salt and pepper. Serve the turkey rolls with the sauce and freshly chopped basil.

9.43 Vegetable bowl with Provencal pistou

Promotes spleen and liver, reduces blood pressure, strengthens immune system, prevents cancer, reduces radiation damage, forcing spleen, dissolves stagnation. Relieves constipation, strengthens mother milk production.
Cooking time approx. 1 1/2 hours
Calories p. portion: 138
8 portions
Allergens: AGL

Quantity of ingredients:
Tomato 5/8 oz / 200g. (yes)
Olive oil 2 table spoons / 30g. (yes)
Garlic 1 clove / 5g. (recommended)
Toast bread (whole grain) 1 slice / 5g. (yes)
Parmesan 1 oz / 30g. (yes)
Basil (fresh) 1 Bunch / 125g. (yes)
Salt 1 pinch / 2g. (little)
Pepper (ground) 1 pinch / 1g. (little)
Oregano dried 1 teaspoon / 3g. (yes)
Basic recipe for a vegetable soup (nutritious) 3 lbs / 1250g. (yes)
Carrot 3/8 lbs - 6oz / 150g. (yes)
Celery root 1/4 lbs - 4oz / 100g. (yes)
Broccoli 5/8 oz / 200g. (yes)
Fennel 1 piece / 250g. (yes)
Thyme dried 1/2 teaspoon / 2g. (yes)
Oregano dried 1/2 teaspoon / 2g. (yes)
Bay leaf 1 piece / 0,5g. (yes)
Peas, green 1/8 lbs - 2oz / 50g. (yes)
Onion (spring onion) 4 pieces / 80g. (yes)
Potato 1/4 lbs - 4oz / 100g. (yes)

Cooking instructions:
Sauce:
Tear off tomatoes and cut into small pieces. Reduce in a pot with a little
oliv oil, finely chopped garlic. Add 1 slice of dry toasted bread
(crumbed), fresh finely grated Parmesan, finely chopped basil, oregano,
salt and pepper.

Soup:
Boil the vegetable broth according to the basic recipe, add coarsely
sliced carrots, diced celery, diced potatoes, small florets, broccoli, finely
chopped fennel tuber, peas, thyme, oregano and the bay leaf. let cook
10 minutes.

Cut 4 scallions into thin rings, add them and cook another 2 min.

Pour sauce into a soup bowl. First only a few tablespoons. Stir boiling
broth with it, then stir in the soup little by little.

9.44 Vegetable bowl with tofu and curry on rice

Diuretic, reduces blood glucose. Reduces flatulence, supports digestion. Contains ideal herbal mucus, which provides regeneration of the small and large intestinal flora. Reduces blood pressure, strengthens immune system.
Cooking time approx. 30 min
Calories p. portion: 162
6 portions
Allergens: E

Quantity of ingredients:
Olive oil 2 table spoons / 20g. (yes)
Garlic 2 cloves / 3g. (recommended)
Onion white 1 piece / 60g. (yes)
Curry 2 table spoons / 16g. (yes)
Water 2 cup / 500g. (yes)
Turnips 2 pieces / 50g. (yes)
Pumpkin 1 piece / 400g. (yes)
Carrot 1 piece / 100g. (yes)
Parsnip 1 piece / 150g. (yes)
Potato 1 piece / 70g. (yes)
Sweet potato 1 piece / 70g. (yes)
Cauliflower 1/4 piece / 250g. (yes)
Broccoli 1/2 piece / 250g. (yes)
Okra 12 pieces / 200g. (yes)
Soy Tofu 1 piece / 250g. (yes)
Basil 2 table spoons / 12g. (yes)
Salt 1 pinch / 0,5g. (little)

Cooking instructions:
Heat the oil at medium temperature in a large, heavy casserole, add the garlic and onion and sauté with constant stirring. Sprinkle curry powder over it, fry gently for about 5 minutes and make sure that the garlic and curry do not burn. Add the water and heat till it boils. Gradually peel all vegetables, dice and add, starting with the varieties that need the longest cooking time. Once the water has boiled again, reduce the heat and simmer the vegetables for about 15 minutes. When it is almost soft. Add the cauliflower and broccoli florets and the okra and cook the stew for another 10 to 15 minutes. Add the tofu during the last 5 minutes.

Cook the brown rice at the same time: Sprinkle the rice in a medium saucepan with water, salt and cover for about 20 minutes. cook on a low heat. Take from the fire and another 10 min. to let go.

Arrange the stew over the brown rice and sprinkle with basil.

9.45 Whole milk cereal mash

Reduces Inflammation, antiallergic, has a stabilizing effect on the blood circulation, lowers blood glucose and cholesterol.
Cooking time approx. 20 min
Calories p. portion: 205
1 portions
Allergens: AG

Quantity of ingredients:
Cow's milk (whole milk 3.5% fat) 3/4 cup - 6 oz / 200g. (yes)
Water 1/4 cup / 50g. (yes)
Spelled flakes 1/2 oz / 20g. (yes)
Fruit mix juice 1/2 oz / 20g. (recommended)

Cooking instructions:
Boil the milk with the wholegrain flakes and let it swell. Add the pureed fruit.

Switch between wheat, oats and wholemeal spelled flakes, as well as the fruits. So you get a variety of flavors.

10 Effects of food

10.1 Use ingredients: recommendable

Acai powder
Acerola fruit nectar or powder
Aloe juice
Apple (sweet)
Apple juice (natural cloudy)
Apple puree
Apricot
Apricot jam
Banana
Banana (cooking banana)
Bitter Herb liqueur
Blackberry jam
Blueberry jam
Blueberry juice
Chamomile tea
Cherry compote
Compote (fruits of the season)
Cream 10% coffee cream
Currant jam (black)
Elderberry blossom tee
Fish pieces mixed (fresh water)
Fox nut, gorgon nut, makhana
Fruit mix juice
Garlic
Green tea

Hibiscus
Kudzu
Lily bulbs
Lychee in Preserved
Manioc flour
Maple syrup
Mediterranean fish (cod, plaice, haddock, sea eel, mackerel)
Orange jam
Peaches (canned)
Pear juice
Peppermint tea
Reishi mushroom
Soya Cuisine (soy cream)
Strawberry jam
Turmeric (yellow root)
Vegetable juice
Wheat bran
Wheat flour whole grain
Wheat/Rye/Gray-black bread with yeast
Whole grain bread
Wholemeal flour
Wormwood
Yarrow tea

10.2 Use ingredients: yes

Agar agar (kelp)
Agave nectar
Agrimony
Amaranth
Amaranth Pops
Anchovy / Sardine
Angelica root
Anise (Common Fennel)
Apple (sour)
Arrowroot
Artichoke
Asparagus (green or white)
Aubergine
Baking powder
Balm
Bamboo shoots
Banchatee (green tea)
barberry
Barley
Barley flour
Barley grass powder

Barley grouts
Barley malt
Barley not peeled
Basic recipe for a beef soup
Basic recipe for a beef soup (warming)
Basic recipe for a rice soup (Congee)
Basic recipe for a vegetable soup (nutritious)
Basil
Basil (fresh)
Bay leaf
Bean oil
Bearberry leaf
Beef fillet
Beef meat
Beef meat (calf)
Beer (alcohol-free)
Beer (alcohol-reduced)
Bitter Lemon
Bitter orange peel
Black caraway

Black fungus mushroom
Black tea
Blackberry leaves
Blackthorn (Sloe)
Blue mallow tee
Boletus mushroom
Borage
Borage oil
Boxhorn clover seeds
Bread roll
Bread with carob kernel flour
Breadcrumbs (wheat bread, bread roll)
Brie cheese
Broccoli
Brussels sprouts
Buckbean
Buckwheat
Buckwheat (roasted) Kasha
Buckwheat whole grain
Bulgur (cereals)
Burdock root tea
Butter (half fat)
Butter organic
Buttermilk
Calamari
Camembert
Capers in olive oil
Cardamom
Carob flour, St. john's bread
Carp
Carrot
Carrot (Early Carrot)
Carrot juice without sugar
Cauliflower
Celery root
Celery sticks
Cereal coffee
Chamomile
Champignon
Channa-Dal
Chanterelle
Chard
Chenpi (chinese tangerine bowl)
Chervil
Chervil dried
Chestnut puree
Chestnuts
Chicken meat
Chickweed
Chinese cabbage
Chinese pearl barley
Chives
Chlorella (fresh water)
Chrysanthemum blossom tea

Cinnamon ground
Cinnamon sticks
Clove
Cocoa
Cod
Codfish
Coffee
Coix (seeds) YiYi Ren
Cola drink
Coriander
Coriander (fresh)
Corn
Corn (fast polenta)
Corn (roasted)
Corn flour
Corn germ oil
Corn Grease (Polenta)
Corn silk tea
Corn starch
Cottage cheese
Couscous
Cow's milk (1.5% fat)
Cow's milk (whole milk 3.5% fat)
Crab
Cranberry
Cranberry jam
Cranberry juice
Cream sour 10%
Creamer
Créme fraiche cheese
Cress
Crispbread
Crucian
Cucumber
Cucumber (bitter)
Cucumber (spicy cucumber)
Cumin (Caraway seed)
Curcuma
Curd cheese 20%
Currant jam (red)
Curry
Curry paste red
Daisy
Dandelion (young plants)
Dandelion juice
Dandelionroots tea
Dashi
Deer meat
Deer meat
Deer's Bones
Deer's kidneys
Dill
Duck (heart)
Duck (slaughtered)

Ducks egg
Dulse (seaweed)
Dyer's broom herb
Edam cheese
Elderberries
Emmental cheese
Evening primrose oil
Fennel
Fennel seeds ground
Fennel tea
Fenugreek (Trigonella foenum-graecum)
Feta cheese
Feta cheese
Fig
Fish innards
Fish remains
Fish sauce
Flounder
Flower pollen
Fresh cheese
Fresh cheese with herbs
Freshwater crab
Freshwater fish
Fructose (glucose)
Galangal
Garam Masala powder
Gelatin white
Gelee Royal
Gentian root
Gentian root tea
Ginger oil
Ginger powder
Ginseng
Ginseng root
Goat
Goat and sheep's milk
Goat cheese
Goose
Goose blood
Goose egg
Goose parts
Gorgonzola
Gouda cheese
Gourd
Grape juice white
Grapefruit dried peel
Grapeseed oil
Grass carp
Green spelt
Ground
Ground caraway
Halibut (Flatfish)
Hawthorn

Herbal tea mix
Herbs bitter
Herbs of Provence
Herbs various
Herbs wild
Hibiscus tea
Hijiki
Hokkaido pumpkin
Honey
Hop
Horehound leaves
Horse meat
Hyssop
Jasmine blossoms tee
Jellyfish
Juniper berry
Kalmus
Kefir
King Solomon's-seal
Kohlrabi
Kombu seaweed (Saccharina japonica)
Kukicha tea
Kumquats
Ladyfingers
Lamb meat
Lamb shoulder
Lavender blossoms
Leek
Lemon Balm (dried)
Lemon Balm (fresh)
Lemon peel
Lemongrass
Licorice root tea
Lime blossom tea
Linseed
Linseed (crushed)
Linseed oil
Liver smoothing tea
Longane
Loquate / Japanese medlar
Lotus roots
Lotus seeds
Lovage
Lovage seeds
Lye roll
Mallow (Malva sylvestris) blossom tea
Malt
Mango juice
Mare's milk
Margarine
Marjoram
Medlar
Millet flakes
Mineral water

Miso
Miso black (fermented)
Miso paste (soy bean paste)
Mixed Pickles
Mold cheese
Morel (black, dried)
Morel, dried
Mozzarella
Mu Erh Mushroom
Muesli
Mulled Wine Spice
Mullet
Multi-grain bread (gray bread)
Mung bean sprouting
Mussels
Mustard
Mustard medium hot
Mustard sweet
Mutton
Mutton
Nasturtium (nose-twister or nose-tweaker)
Nectarine
Nettles
Noodles (wheat) with egg
Noodles (wheat, lasagne) with egg
Noodles (wheat, ribbon noodles) with egg
Noodles (wheat, spaghetti) with egg
Noodles (whole grain) with egg
Nori, purple seaweed, red algae
Nutmeg
Oat
Oat flakes (whole grain)
Oat flakes roasted
Oat flour
Oat fusion (baby food)
Oat meal
Oat milk
Octopus
Octopus
Okra
Olive oil
Olives
Olives green
Onion (shallot)
Onion (spring onion)
Onion read
Onion white
Orange blossom
Orange dried peel
Orange grated peel
Orange peel
Oregano dried

Oregano fresh
Oyster mushroom
Oyster shell powder
Oysters
Palm oil
Parmesan
Parsley
Parsley root
Parsnip
Passion blossoms tea
Passion fruit
Peanut (roasted)
Peanut oil
Pearl barley
Pearl barley
Peas
Peas, green
Pepper powder (hot)
Peppermint
Pepperoni
Peppers
Peppers (rose peppers)
Peppers (sweet)
Peppers powder
Perch
Pheasant
Pickle
Pigeon
Pigeon egg
Pimento
Pineapple (from a can)
Plaice
Poppy
Potato
Potato (mealy)
Potato flour
Prickly pear
Processed cheese 12%
Psyllium seed
Pudding powder vanilla
Puff pastry
Pumpernickel (dark bread)
Pumpkin
Pumpkin seed oil
Quince
Quinoa
Rabbit
Rabbit (wild)
Rabbit meat
Radicchio
Radish (white, green, purple-red)
Radish black
Radish leaves
Rapeseed oil

Raspberry jam
Raspberry leaf tea
Red beet
Red cabbage
Rhubarb
Ribworttea
Rice (fragrance)
Rice (Gaoliang / Sorghum)
Rice (whole grain)
Rice Basmati
Rice black
Rice flour
Rice long grain rice
Rice malt
Rice mash
Rice noodles
Rice red
Rice round grain
Rice starch
Rice sticky
Rice sweet
Rice variety any
Rice wild (nature rice)
Rose blossom tea
Rose hip
Rose hip tea
Rose leaf tea
Rosefish
Rosemary
Rusk
Rye
Rye flour
Rye wholemeal bread
Safflower (Dyer's thistle / Hong Hua)
Saffron
Sage
Sago (cereals)
Sake
Salsify
Sauerkraut (cutted cabbage fermented)
Savory
Savoy cabbage / kale
Sea buckthorn
Sea cucumber
Seacrab
Sesame oil
Sesame oil roasted
Sesame paste (Tahini)
Shark
Sheep's milk
Sheep's milk yoghurt
Shiitake, dried
Shrimp
Shrimps

Skim milk powder
Slug
Sorrel
Sour cream 15% fat
Sour milk
Sour milk cheese 20%
Sourdough
Soy flour
Soy noodles
Soy sauce
Soy Tofu
Soybean milk
Soybean oil
Soybeans, blacks, fermented
Spelled (Dark) bread
Spelled flakes
Spelled grain
Spelled semolina
Spelled wholemeal flour
Spinach
Spiny lobsters
Spurdog (spiny dogfish, Schillerlocken)
St. Benedict's thistle, blessed thistle,
holy thistle, spotted thistle
Star anise
Stevia (candyleaf, sweetleaf)
Strawberry Juice
Sugar fructose - fruit sugar
Sugar glucose - grapes sugar
Sugar Milk Sugar
Sugar substitute (sweetener)
Sunflower oil
Supplementary nutrition
Sweet potato
Tarragon (Estragon)
Tea mixture uric acid lowering
Thistle oil
Thyme
Thyme dried
Toast bread (whole grain)
Tomato
Tomato juice
Tomato paste
Tomato puree
Tonic Water
Topinambur
Trout
Trout (smoked)
Truffle
Tsampa (roasted barley flour)
Tuna
Turkey breast meat
Turkey ham
Turnip

Turnips
Umeboshi paste
Umeboshi plums (Japanese apricots)
Valerian
Vanilla
Vanilla pod
Vanilla powder
Vanilla sugar natural
Vinegar (Apple vinegar)
Vinegar (Red wine vinegar)
Vinegar Aceto Balsamico
Vinegar Aceto Balsamico white
Wakame
Walnut oil
Walnuts roasted
Water
Water hot
Wax gourd
Wheat
Wheat bulgur
Wheat flakes
Wheat flour

Wheat germ oil
Wheat semolina
Wheat semolina for children
Wheatgrass juice
Wheatgrass powder
Whey
White cabbage
Whitefish
Wild boar meat
Wild garlic (garlic spinach)
Wild herbs
Wormwood herb
Yam root, yam root tuber
Yarrow
Yeast
Yew nut
Yoghurt vanilla
Yogi tea
Yogurt (natural, 1.5% fat)
Yogurt (natural, 3.5% fat)
Zucchini

10.3 Use ingredients: little

Adzuki beans
Apricot nectar
Apricots
Apricots juice
Basic recipe for a chicken soup
(warming)
Basic recipe for a duck soup
Basic recipe for a fish soup
Beans (green, fresh)
Beef bone marrow
Beef heart
Beef heart (calf)
Beef kidney
Beef liver
Beef lungs (calf)
Beef meatbones
Beef Oxtail pieces
Beef soup meat
Beef stomach
Beer (Pils)
Beer (Top-fermented German dark
beer)
Berry juice
Bitter liqueur
Black beans
Black-eyed peas
Broad beans (thick beans)
Brown ale

Bush beans
Butter beans white
Campari
Cantaloupe
Carambola (Star fruit)
Caviar
Cherry juice
Chicken Blood
Chicken egg
Chicken egg white
Chicken heart
Chicken liver
Chicken stomach
Chicken yolk
Chickpeas
Chocolate
Chocolate (Diabetic)
Clarified butter
Clementines
Coconut fat
Cola drink (low calorie)
Cooking oil
Cranberry
Cream (30% fat)
Cream sour 20%
Cream sour 30%
Cream, sweet 30%
Curd cheese 40%

Currant (black)
Currant juice (black)
Dates red
Eel
Fernet Branca (herbal bitter liqueur)
French beans
Fresh cheese from soya
Fruit tea
Gail plum
Ginger fresh
Ginkgo fruit
Ginseng liqueur
Goat and sheep's blood
Goat and sheep's brain
Goat and sheep's liver
Goat and sheep's stomach
Goose fat
Grape juice red
Guava
Honey wine (Met)
Kaki plum
Kidney beans (red)
Kiwi
Lamb bones
Lamb kidneys
Lamb liver
Lemon
Lemon juice
Lentils
Lentils black
Lentils red
Lentils yellow
Lima beans
Lime
Lobster
Luo Han Guo fruit
Lychee
Lychee liqueur
Mackerel
Mango
Margarine (diet)
Martini
Mascarpone cheese
Millet
Mirabelle plum
Mung bean
Mustard Dijon
Orange
Papaya
Peaches
Pear
Pepper (ground)
Pepper Cayenne
Pepper white (ground)

Peppercorns
Pig blood
Pineapple juice without sugar
Pinto beans speckled
Pistachios
Plum
Pork Bacon
Pork brain
Pork fat (lard)
Pork ham
Pork ham cooked
Pork ham smoked
Pork heart
Pork kidneys
Pork knuckle
Pork Lard
Pork liver
Pork lung
Pork marrow bones
Pork meat
Pork sausage (Bratwurst) Pork skin
Pork stomach
Pork/beef sausage (smoked)
Pork's intestine
processed cheese 30%
Prosecco
Quail
Quail egg
Rabbit liver
Radish horseradish
Red berry (without sugar)
Red wine
Rum
Salmon
Salt
Salt (herbal)
Sesame, white
Sherry (whine)
Soy Tofu smoked
Soybeans
Soybeans, black
Soybeans, yellow
Spirit
Strawberries
Sugar - icing sugar
Sugar brown
Sugar candy white
Sugar cane sugar
Sugar molasses
Sugar palm sugar
Sugar white
Tangerine
Watermelon
Wheat beer

Wheat flatbread/pita bread
White beans
White bread (baguette)
White bread (pretzel sticks)
White bread (roll)

White bread (wheat bread)
White breadcrumbs
White dumpling bread (wheat bread cut into chunks)
White wine

10.4 Do not use contra-acting foods

Almond
Almond marzipan
Almond milk
Almond puree
Apricot dried
Avocado
Batavia
Berries of the season
Blackberry dried (unripe fruit)
Blackberry´s
Blueberry
Blueberry dried
Bocksdorn fruits (Fructus Lycii, Goji, goji berry Brazil nuts
Cashews
Cherry
Cherry (sour)
Chicory
Chili (pod or ground)
Clementine
Coconut flakes
Coconut grated
Coconut meat
Coconut milk
Cranberries
Currant (red)
Currant (white)
Currants (black)
Currants (red)
Dates dried
Eel smoked
Endive salad
Fig dried
Gooseberry
Grapefruit (Pomelo)
Grapefruit juice
Grapes red

Grapes white
Greengage
Hazelnuts
Herring
Iceberg lettuce
Lamb's lettuce
Lamb's lettuce
Leaf salads (bitter)
Lettuce
Mayonnaise 50%
Mayonnaise 80%
Mulberry fruit
Mustard seeds
Orange juice
Peanut butter
Peanuts
Pepperoni, red, pitted, halved
Pepperoni, yellow, pitted, halved
Pine nuts
Pineapple
Plum dried
Plums
Pomegranate
Pumpkin seeds
Radish
Raisins
Raspberry
Raspberry dried (immature)
Romaine lettuce / lettuce salad
Rucola
Sesame, black
Sour cherries
Sunflower seeds
Tabasco
Tomato dried
Walnuts
Wild strawberries

11 Herbs and their effects

11.1 Basil

It has a beneficial effect on flatulence and nausea, relaxing and soothing.

Good to fight emphysema, bronchitis, whooping cough, high blood pressure, headache, mouth odor, warts, hiccup, gout, migraine.

11.2 Mugwort

Reduces bleeding, alleviates pain. In the kitchen, mugwort is used as a spice for fat food. Since it contains many bitter substances, it boosts fat burning and promotes digestion.

11.3 Savory

Stomach-strengthening, soothing and appetizing. Ideal for prevent colds, strengthens the immun system. In case of incontinence or nocturnal wetting (not for children), put the beans in liquor for libido.

11.4 Dill

The medicinal and spice herb has an antispasmodic effect and stimulates gastric juice production. Good to fight flatulence. Antispasmodic for gastrointestinal discomfort.

11.5 Coriander

The essential oils are appetizing, digestive, cramping and soothing in stomach and intestinal disorders.

11.6 Herbs various

Appetizing, lots of trace elements and vitamins

11.7 Chives

Bactericide, prevents cancer, strengthens gastric juice production, promotes digestion and blood circulation, promotes growth, triggers stagnation.

11.8 Lily bulbs

Calms nerves, good to fight scaly skin. The onions and the petals are added to ointments in the Orient, which can heal muscles and tendons. White lily (astringent).

11.9 Oregano fresh

It has an anti-digestive, calming and nerve-strengthening effect, helps to fight cramping stomach and intestinal disorders. The ingredient Carvacrol has an anti-inflammatory effect.

11.10 Oregano dried

It has an anti-digestive, calming and nerve-strengthening effect, helps to fight cramping stomach and intestinal disorders. The ingredient Carvacrol has an anti-inflammatory effect.

11.11 Parsley

Stimulates liver function, detoxifies. Forces urinating. Relieves flatulence. Digestive and menstrual stimulating, birth-accelerating, memory-enhancing, blood-purifying, skin-smoothing.

11.12 Peppermint

Relaxes, frees the lungs and the nose (inhale), regulates the cycle. Stimulates bile flow and bile production, antispasmodic in gastrointestinal disorders, antimicrobial and antiviral.

11.13 Rosemary

Promotes digestion, relieves bloating, strengthens lung, spleen and kidney. Affects the circulation and nerves. Appetizing. Baths help to fight circulatory disorders as well as with gout and rheumatism.

11.14 Black caraway

Detoxifying, immunoregulatory. In addition, the oil should stimulate the formation of bone marrow cells and generally protect body cells from viruses.

11.15 Thyme dried

Disinfecting. It stimulates the blood circulation, increases the appetite and helps to digest fat meat better. Strengthens lungs and spleen (TCM).

11.16 King Solomon's-seal

Used to repair wounds or damaged tissue. Good to fight dry cough, earlier also tuberculosis and dysentery, as well as diarrhea and hemorrhoids.

11.17 Yam root, yam root tuber

Solves cramps (in the gastrointestinal tract). Digestive through increased bile production. Anti-inflammatory in rheumatic diseases.
Mucolytic agent for coughing. Relief of menopausal symptoms.

11.18 Lemongrass

Reduction of flatulence, antimicrobial, appetizing. Prevention of influenza. Good to fight infections in the mouth and throat.

12 Basics of Nutrition

The basic principles of nutrition described herein are general recommendations. They are not aimed at a specific form of therapy. Recommendations concerning a therapy have priority.

12.1 Nutrition

Regular meals in a relaxed atmosphere. A warm breakfast is considered a good start into the day.
The main meals ought to be taken for lunch – supper in the early evening. Pay attention to feeling hungry or sated: don't eat too much nor remain hungry is the rule
Prepare the meals freshly from natural, regional products. Frozen, heat-conserved, industrially prepared or foodstuffs cooked in the microwave oven are rejected.
Choice of foodstuffs according to the season: more cooling food in summer, more warming food in winter.
Eat cooked food at least twice a day. Food and drinks ought to be lukewarm, never ice-cold or hot.
Raw vegetables, briefly cooked vegetables, freshly squeezed juices and mineral water are not recommended. Milk and dairy products are only included in the diet if they don't cause problems.
Don't use therapeutic recipes over a longer period without consulting your doctor or therapist.

Varied food
Enjoy the diversity of foodstuffs. Characteristics of a balanced nutrition are variety, suitable combination and a balanced quantity of rich and low energy foodstuffs (on one hand avoiding undersupply with essential nutrients and on the other hand to take to many undesirable substances).

A lot of Cereal Products - and Potatoes
Bread, pasta, rice, cereal flakes (best wholemeal) as well as potatoes contain almost no fat, but many vitamins, mineral nutrients, trace elements, roughage and secondary plant substances. These foodstuffs ought to be taken with low-fat side dishes.

Vegetables and Fruit – „Take Five" every day ...
5 portions of vegetables and fruit a day, as fresh as possible, briefly cooked, or maybe one portion as a juice – ideal as a side dish to every meal as well as snack between meals: Thus a lot of vitamins, mineral nutrients as well as roughage and secondary plant substances

Daily milk and dairy products

Milk and Dairy Products every Day, once or twice per Week Fish; meat, sausages as well as eggs moderately. These foodstuffs contain valuable nutrients like calcium in the milk, iodine selenium and omega-3 fat acids in saltwater fish. Meat is favorable due to its high content of disposable iron and the vitamins B1, B6 and B12. Quantities of 300 – 600 g meat and sausage per week are sufficient. Prefer low-fat products, especially in meat- and dairy products.

Low-fat and fatty Foodstuffs

Fat supplies us with essential fat acids and fatty foodstuffs contain also fat-soluble vitamins. Fat is high in energy; therefore much fat in the food may cause overweight, possibly also cancer. Too many saturated fat acids may further a tendency for cardio-vascular diseases in the long term. Prefer vegetable oils and fats (e.g. rapeseed-, olive-, soya-oils and solid fats produced therefrom). Beware of invisible fat in meat- and dairy products, pastry and sweets as well as in fast-food and convenience foods. 70 – 90 g fat per day is sufficient.

Moderately Sugar and Salt

Take sugar and foods/drinks containing various kinds of sugar (e.g. glucose syrup) only occasionally. Use herbs and spices as well as a little salt creatively. Prefer salt containing iodine.

Plenty of Liquids

Water is absolutely essential. Drink 1-2 l liquids every day. Prefer water (with or without gas) and other low-calorie drinks. Alcoholic drinks should not be taken.

Tasty Dishes, carefully cooked

Cook the meals with as low temperatures and as short as possible, using little water and fat – this preserves the original taste, keeps the nutrients intact and prevents the production of harmful compounds.

Take time and enjoy the food

Take your Time and enjoy your Food
Eating consciously helps to eat right. The eye enjoys food, too. It's fun, invites to enjoy varied dishes and stimulates the feeling of satiety.

Watch your Weight and stay in Motion

A balanced diet and a lot of exercise and sport (30 – 60 min/day) are a healthy combination. The right weight furthers well-being and health. Thermals, directional effectiveness, digestive power

There are various criteria for judging the effectiveness of herbs and foodstuffs.

The use of certain herbs and ingredients is based on observations of the effects on the body which these foodstuffs, herbs and spices show after having eaten them. The medical science has developed following system: Every ingredient or herb has a directional effectiveness. Furthermore, there are herbs which have a special effect on certain organs.

The basic condition for a healthy metabolism is to obtain sufficient energy from food and that the digestive process doesn't use too much energy. An easily digestible meal makes content and sated, doesn't cause flatulence and fatigue after the meal. The perfect spices increase the healthiness of our meals. Very often, just small doses of herbs and spices will suffice. They are not used to make us sated, but to help our digestive organs to digest the food.

12.2 Recipes

The recipes list the ingredients to be used and the cooking instructions show how the dish is prepared. The list of ingredients shows the concerned quantities as well as the relevance for the therapy. If you find „less than mentioned", try to comply or find an alternative from the „list of recommended foodstuffs". Mostly it shall result just in a small change of taste when you simply avoid this ingredient.

Mild cooking methods: boiling, stewing, poaching, steaming
Strong cooking methods: barbecuing, roasting, frying, smoking
Balanced cooking methods: deep-frying, baking brick
Deep-freezing and warming in the microwave oven should be avoided (denaturalization).

12.3 Foodstuffs

Foodstuffs have an effect on body and soul like medicinal herbs, only a very much milder one. Dietary advice is mainly based on regional foodstuffs. The knowledge about the effects of each foodstuff and the knowledge, when which foodstuff shall be used, is based on the orthodoschool of medicine. Use ecologic-organic products, if possible. As everything should be cooked for a long time due to a better digestability and very rarely eaten raw, the food agrees with everyone.

The classification of the foodstuffs according to their effect on the body is the basis in order to achieve a harmonious status of health.

Dietary advisors do not recommend certain foodstuffs for everyone. The individual diet is tailor-made for the individual constitution.

Buy only fresh and ripe fruit and vegetables. You ought to leave unripe fruit and vegetables and such with brown spots and wilted leaves behind in the market. In this case take deep-frozen goods (never ready-to-serve dishes!). Fruit and vegetables are deep-frozen immediately after harvesting and often contain more vitamins and minerals than the goods from the vegetable shelf. Whereas conserved or tinned goods contain very much less biological substances. Also, salt, sugar and others are mostly added to the latter. Never leave the foodstuffs in the water after washing them to avoid that many vital substances get drowned. Clean salads, fruit and vegetables immediately before serving.

Please make sure of the hygienic processing of foodstuffs. Clean your salads, fruit and vegetables carefully. When cooking with meat, prepare all ingredients first and then process the meat products. Clean the worktop and tools very carefully. Wooden surfaces ought to be treated with a mild disinfectant regularly in order to reduce germination.

Store fruit and vegetables separately, if possible. Harvested fruit and vegetables are still alive and emit e.g. ethylene gas, which makes other products ripen and age faster. Keep meat and fish in the closed packaging or store them in the fridge in closed containers.

12.4 Herbs

There are some basic rules for storing medicinal herbs. On principle, herbs must be protected from direct sunlight, humidity and heat.

Containers for the storage of herbs may be glasses, ceramic jars and even plastic containers. However, plastic is a rather unsuitable material and should only be a short-term solution. In case of glass containers, use a dark material.

Medicinal herbs cannot be kept for any long period. The shelf life of herbs is limited. However, it can be prolonged with suitable storage. The place should be dark, rather cool and absolutely dry. A wooden medicine cabinet, placed not directly next to a source of heat, would be ideal. Never buy large quantities of herbs so as not to have to throw them away. Label the container with the name of the herb and the date of harvesting or processing.

13 Other dietic-books

The following syndromes of dietetics, TCM or for a therapy supplement for cancer are available.

Dietetics

E001. Nutrition of the infant - baby food
E002. Nutrition during lactation
E003. Nutrition in old age
E004. Nutrition of children and adolescents
E005. Nutrition of athletes
E006. Light weight
E007. Pregnancy
E008. Full food

Protein and electrolyte - kidneys
E009. (hemodialysis) dialysis treatment
E010. Acute renal failure
E011. Chronic renal insufficiency
E012. Nephrotic syndrome
E013. Kidney stones (nephrolithiasis)

Gastrointestinal tract - pancreas
E014. Acute pancreatitis (inflammation of the pancreas)
E015. Chronic pancreatitis (inflammation of the pancreas)

Gastrointestinal tract - small intestine and large intestine
E016. Acute obstipation (constipation)
E017. Chronic obstipation (constipation)
E018. Colon irritabile
E019. Diverticulitis
E020. Acquired lactose intolerance (lactose malabsorption)
E021. Fructose malabsorption
E022. Glutensensitive enteropathy (celiac disease)
E023. Colectomy
E024. Short Bowel Syndrome

Gastrointestinal tract - liver, gallbladder, bile ducts
E025. Acute and chronic hepatitis (inflammation of the liver)
E026. Cholelithiasis (bile stones)
E027. fatty liver
E028. cirrhosis

Gastrointestinal tract - Stomach and duodenal intestine
E029. Acute gastritis
E030. Chronic gastritis
E031. Stomach bleeding
E032. Ulcus ventriculi and duodenal ulcer
E033. Condition after gastric surgery

Gastrointestinal tract - oral cavity and esophagus
E034. Stomatitis
E035. Esophageal carcinoma (esophageal cancer)
E036. Refluosophagitis (heartburn)

Special diseases
E037. Phenylketonuria (PKU)
E038. Rheumatic joint diseases

Metabolism
E039. Obesity (overweight)
E040. Diabetes mellitus
E041. Eating disorders (underweight)

Fat metabolism
E042. Hypercholesterolaemia (increased cholesterol level)
E043. Hepatic Encephalopathy

Heart and circulation
E044. Arteriosclerosis (arterial calcification)
E045. Heart insufficiency
E046. Hypertension
E047. Hyperuricaemia and gout

Changed nutrient requirements
E048. In case of fever
E049. For malignant diseases
E050. After burns
E051. Radiation and chemotherapy

CANCER
E100. Pancreatic cancer
E101. Bladder cancer
E102. Blood cancer (leukemia)
E103. Breast cancer
E104. Colorectal cancer
E105. Gastric cancer
E106. Kidney cancer
E107. Esophageal cancer

TCM
E200. Bladder - moisture heat in the bladder
E201. Bladder - moisture and cold in the bladder
E202. Bladder - emptiness and cold in the bladder
E203. Large intestine - external cold affects the large intestine
E204. Large intestine - moisture heat in the large intestine
E205. Large intestine - heat blocks the intestine II acute
E206. Large intestine - dryness of the colon
E207. Large intestine - Yang deficiency (cold)
E208. Heart - Blood insufficiency
E209. Heart - Blood stagnation
E210. Heart - Fire
E211. Heart - Hot mucus clogs the heart pores

E212. Heart - Cold mucus clogs the heart pores
E213. Heart - Qi deficiency
E214. Heart - Yang deficiency
E215. Heart - Yin deficiency
E216. Liver - Ascending Liver Yang
E217. Liver - Blood deficiency
E218. Liver - Blood stagnation
E219. Liver - Moisture heat in liver and gall bladder
E220. Liver - Fire
E221. Liver - Gall bladder Qi-Empty
E222. Liver - Cold in the liver meridian
E223. Liver - Qi stagnation
E224. Liver - Wind
E225. Liver - Wind with ascending liver Yang
E226. Liver - Wind with blood anemic
E227. Liver - Wind with extreme heat
E228. Lung - Qi deficiency
E229. Lung - Mucus-moisture in the lungs
E230. Lung - Mucus-heat in the lungs
E231. Lung - Mucus-cold in the lungs
E232. Lung - Dryness of the lungs
E233. Lung - Wind-heat attacks the lungs
E234. Lung - Wind-cold affects the lungs
E235. Lung - Yin deficiency
E236. Stomach - Bloodstagnation
E237. Stomach - Fire
E238. Stomach - Cold with liquid
E239. Stomach - Nutrition stagnation
E240. Stomach - Qi deficiency
E241. Stomach - Rebellious Qi
E242. Stomach - Yin Emptiness
E243. Spleen - Heat and moisture attack the spleen
E244. Spleen - Coldness and moisture affects the spleen
E245. Spleen - Qi deficiency
E246. Spleen - Qi deficiency + Declining spleen Qi
E247. Spleen - Qi deficiency + spleen does not control the blood
E248. Spleen - Yang deficiency
E249. Kidney - Heart and kidney no longer communicate
E250. Kidney - Jing deficiency
E251. Kidney - Kidneys cannot receive the Qi
E252. Kidney - Qi is not stable
E253. Kidney - Yang deficiency
E254. Kidney - Yin deficiency

For further information visit di-book.com.